Dear Friend:

Glad you're able to come along on this journey and share my movie. Our times are strange and scary, as you know. Each day brings news. We all seem in for it now and ought to stick together.

And hope? Love? Respite from fear? That's what this paper movie is about. Just the facts, and other mysteries.

My 90 photographs are untricked, mostly made by natural light with a small inexpensive camera.

Virginia is Virginia Adams, widow of Ansel. Rick, Leilani, Dan Rather and everyone else seen or named are also real. Except Larissa and the Stranger, who are fictional--or perhaps not.

# JOURNEY TO LAND'S END

---

a paper movie by
## LOU STOUMEN

---

CELESTIALARTS

*Berkeley, California*

for JULIA SIEBEL

and for
ELENA
JOAQUIN
LUIS
MAURICIO
ROBERT

Journey To Land's End
was designed by Marissa Roth
and Lou Stoumen at
Hand Press, Los Angeles

Text and Photographs
**Copyright © 1988 by LOU STOUMEN**
All rights reserved. No part of this book may be
reproduced in any form, except for brief reviews,
without written permission from the publisher:
Celestial Arts, P.O. Box 7123, Berkeley, CA 94707. This
softcover edition printed by Malloy Lithographing, Inc. in
Ann Arbor, MI from halftone negatives made by Singer
Printing Co., Petaluma, CA. A limited edition in hardcover was also printed by Singer in its PhotoLustro
process. Manufactured in the United States of America.

Library of Congress Cataloging-in-Publication Data

Stoumen, Louis Clyde
  Journey to land's end: a paper movie/by Lou Stoumen
  I. Photography, Artistic. 2. Photography, Documentary.
I. Title. TRG54. 5766 1988
813 .52--dc19
L of C Catalogue Card Number: 87-27232
International Standard Book Numbers:
  0-89087-520-0 (Hardcover)
  0-89087-521-9 (Paperback)

# THE SOUNDTRACK

*The author's thanks and indebtedness
to actors, friends, helpers and
masters are heartfelt.   Some are
indicated in the Credits on page 159.*

# 1 CHANGES

**All of us would remember**

**in darker times**

that one golden day
when the rising sun made everything new
when each breath tasted of surprise
when love sweet love walked close forever.

Larissa, who had visions, remembered such a day.
It was golden. Her eighteenth birthday.
The very day before all the Changes started.
It was also the day she said goodbye to Rick
her first and last lover.

I *don't understand,* said Rick. W*hy?*

I *don't know,* Larissa answered.

*Give me a clue, damn it!* he said.
Larissa's eyes misted over.

It *has something to do with time,* she said.
*Maybe love should never be named.*

Larissa touched him with a final kiss
and walked through trees.

Rick watched her go.
S*hit!* he said, and kicked the fence.

I can tell you about Larissa, **her father said.**
She was born beautiful and too wise.
Her mother and I worried from the start.
Larissa never wanted to play with kids.
Most of her friends were adults
or characters from books.

Or trees, **her mother added,** she talks to trees.
She likes the company of teachers, medical doctors
nuns and people who make things with their hands.
We had to drag her to Disneyland.
How will such a child find a man
she can be happy with?

Peculiar thing, **her father continued**
Larissa sees through things. She knows.
She sees the end in every beginning.
The skull in her morning mirror.

That afternoon nevertheless
Rick came over for the party.
After we finished Larissa's eighteen-candle cake
we all sat on the porch
and drank iced plum wine spiked with gin.
*Just dandy!* said Cousin George, smacking his lips.
Little Redtop spilled cocacola
over her new pinafore, and cried.
Larissa and Rick talked softly
friendship seemed possible.

Cousin George, who was an actor, told a story.
*After the smoke cleared,* he was saying—
when he let go a sudden heroic fart.

Eyes turned. Little Redtop chirped a giggle.
George surveyed his audience gravely.
*What did you expect?* he inquired, *Beethoven?*

After laughter
we all sat quietly
digested our dinner
and watched the maples
burn red in autumn sunset.

Next morning there were signs.
Tremors of consciousness.
Our animals acted strangely.

My camera began to see things I couldn't.

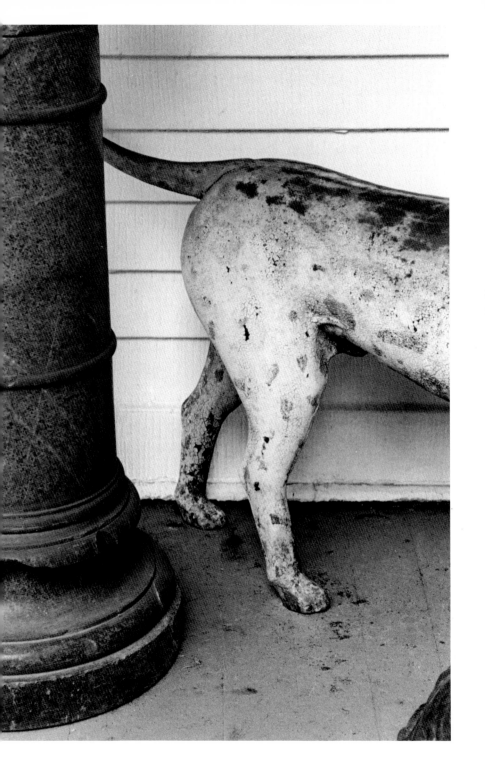

Some of us feared and a few hoped
whatever was coming
would happen soon.

Would the sun explode?
The earth?
Not impossible these days.

It didn't happen that way.
The Changes came on by degrees
seeping like peculiar air
like mutant thought
through our days and dreams.

Among our friends Tyrone went first.
Brushing his teeth that morning
he said to Sally, Hey, I *feel funny!*
He developed a cough
that wouldn't respond to Vicks.

Before the BioTeam got the virus
under partial control
more than 300 died in our community.

We didn't know at the time
there were other outbreaks internationally.
They continue.

Betty Sue, walking to work
was shot dead by a sniper in a pickup.

The SwaTeam took her killer alive
in the Safeway parking lot, cooled him with a StunGun.

That was after he murdered
84 shoppers, clerks and kids.
Used an *Uzi* machine gun, a .45 Colt
and a combat knife.   Betty Sue got hers
from the 30.06 Remington he kept in his cab.

He was crazy of course.   Unemployed former military man.
Said he didn't know Betty Sue
just liked the way she walked.
Said he didn't know any of the Safeway 84
except the assistant manager
who fired him two years ago.

While he still held hostages
he tried to bargain
to tell his story on network TV.

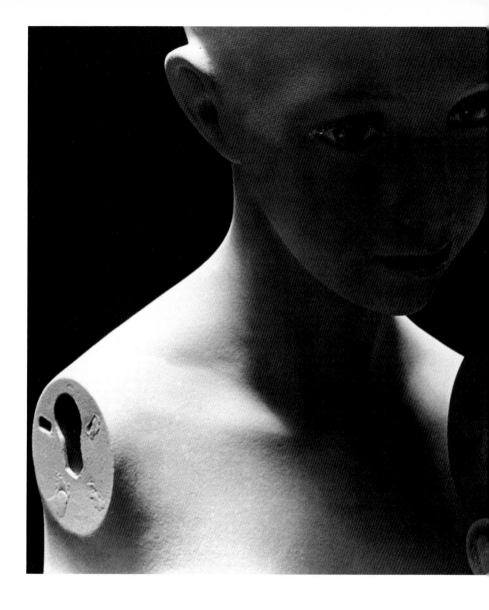

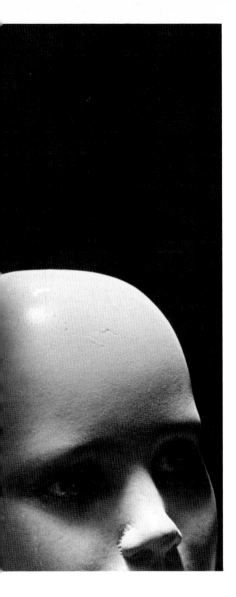

Sam and Ivan were the toughest kids in the neighborhood.
They didn't like each other much
but had to share the same turf.

Coming home from kindergarten one day
arguing who owned it
they strangled a cat.

AR'TRIES ARE RED;
VIOLENCE IS TRUE—
SHOW ME A KNIFE
AND I'LL STICK IN YOU

Our trials are red
our failures are blue
violence is death
That there's peace in love is true

Thank God
there
still
ignora

## 2 LEAVING

**Alexandra was one who remained serene.**

**At first.**

*I've got meditations to do, **she said.***
*And my painting. Please don't bother me*
*with negative thoughts.*

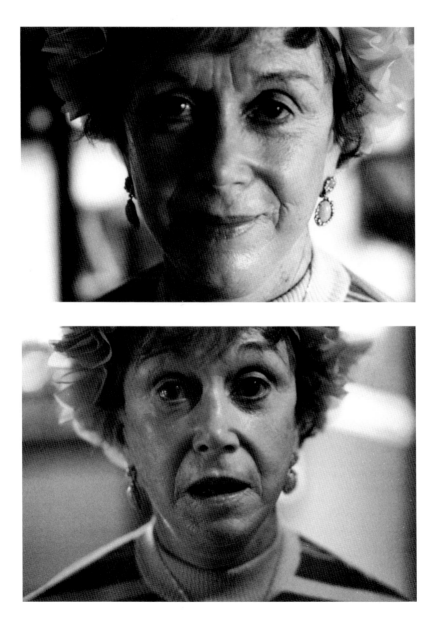

**Teshome was straightforward.**
*I'm confused and frightened,* **he said.**
*But also hopeful. There are forces in the world*
*for decency. They may prevail.*




Why are some people white and some
so dark? **asked Little Redtop.**

Who knows? **her mother replied.**
That's the way things are.

Mommie, **Little Redtop insisted,**
if you kiss a black person
does he taste like chocolate pudding?

Oh hush, **Mommie said**
do you taste like vanilla?

**Fritzie was unflappable.**

*Life goes on,* **she said.**

*Let's eat first.*
*Later we'll do aerobics*
*and play around in the hot tub.*
*Then we can worry.*

**But Don had a hunch**
**we'd better look outside.**

When we saw the trees were dying
Fritzie had to agree something was wrong.
Besides
the electricity had shut itself off
food in the freezer was all spoiled
and the computer was down down down.

*How are we expected to cope?* **Fritzie wanted to know.**
*Our menus, budgets and schedules*
*are all programmed inside that stupid machine.*

**Government experts made an announcement.**

*Don't worry,* **they said.**
*Things aren't bad, they're good.*
*The President has more information than you do.*
*We're working on a plan.*

To reassure everyone, the Government held
a MissileLaunchOpenHousePhotoOpportunity.

Thousands of silver birds nested at Freedom AirBase.
Biggest were the MX Peacemakers
each with several heads
any one of which could kill a small country.

For us they launched only a SpySat.
From 300 miles up
it could finger other missiles in space
or see through earth's surface.
It could make sharp photographs
of oil under rocks
a tank in a forest
or a spoon in soup.

The launch shook earth and air.
O*ooooooooooh*!. . said Marie and everybody.

Marie was an intellectually curious
but lonely
young woman.

She had to ask one of the handsome soldierboys
*How come the mushroom cloud is upside down?*
She hoped he would ask for her phone number.

But the soldierboy remained professional.
*You see, Miss,* he replied smartly
*you only get rightside up configuration*
*from incoming rounds.*

**Life in the world went on, and on . . .**

Rick found himself a new love.
Leilani was Hawaiian, Italian and American.
She taught High School English.

She and Rick first noticed the Changes
while watching television.

During the news Dan got rather strange.
As if alien genius engineers
had taken over the network.

Rick got rather strange two.

But love soon maid him ryght again.

**Don Ruther reported weird weather**
**over the world's capitol cities.**

*Whenever you are, better find go,* **he explained.**
*Like now, before the Big Commercial comes on.*

*Rick!* **shrieked Leilani, zipping up her stretch jeans**
*I'm scared!*

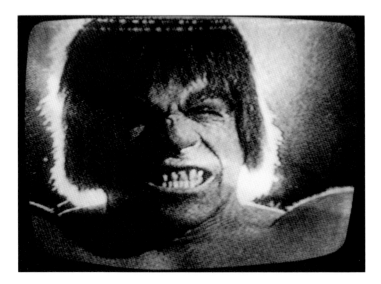

**Rick had leadership qualities.**
**He'd gone from grunt to captain in Vietnam**
**and was a chicken colonel in the Reserves.**

*You drive, dear. Quick!* **Rick said.**
*To the Armory! We've got to organize*
*TemporaryEmergencyTransport!*

65

We drove all day and into night
windows closed
getting away from the troubles
the places where breathing was difficult.

**Everyone searched for a safe way.**
**There was no useful radio information.**

**Road signs got unreliable, crazy.**
*JERICHO,* **they read.** *GOMORRAH. PLEIKU.*
*ATLANTIS. PEPSI. MANAGUA. POMPEII.*
*MENE MENE TEKEL UPHARSIN.*

By nightfall we reached Coastway.
The air was breathable.

Our hope was to turn inland
find safety in some green village.
But the flow of cars began
to fibrillate.

There was *cardiac* arrest.

People walked the immobile rows
asking for gas, water, blankets, food for the kids.

Others with flashlights, tire irons and
handguns soon required whiskey, tobacco
cocaine, women. They took anything they could
drink, smoke, drop, shoot, snort or disrobe.

Down the rows we heard laughter, anger, screams.
We managed to abandon our wheels, some of us
and set out on foot across country.

# 3 JOURNEY

When dawn broke the world open again
the Changes were everywhere.

Marie met a Stranger with a baby on his back.
*Why is it so quiet here?* **she asked him.** *Is this history?*

The Stranger regarded Marie closely.
She had active eyes, an earnest friendly face
and gracefullness.

*It's a time of testing,* **the Stranger said.**
*Then would you give me the baby?* **Marie asked.**

**The Stranger hesitated.** *I don't think so*
**he said.** *You're not ready yet.*

Marie's eyes widened even more, and dropped tears.
Was it so obvious that at thirty-one
she was still a virgin?

*Don't cry,* **the Stranger said,** *it's not worth it.*
*See, the baby is dead.*

**Larissa comforted Marie, took her hand.**

*You asked about history,* **Larissa said.**

Honey, it's too late.   All that's crumbling away.

History has turned out to be

proud angry men wrapped in flags.

*That sounds subversive to me,* **said the Stranger**
*if not obscene. No wonder you're not married.*
*Because if only one knows where to look*
*there's plenty of civilization still available.*
*Books! Billboards! Game shows on TV!*

*What I suggest we do is consult*
*Certified Wise Men.*

**We did.**

**They all told us what we already knew.**
**But more clearly.**

Detach yourself from desire, **the Wise Men said.**
In the beginning was the Word.
God is love. God is dead.
Do unto others before they undo you.
Thou shalt not kill.   Smite the infidel!
All men are brothers, women somewhat less.

Be chaste.   Use it or lose it.
Usury is sin.   Live off interest.
Make no graven images, or photographs.
Peace through strength.   Turn the other cheek.
Arbeit macht frei.   Gather ye rosebuds.
Plan ahead.   Be here now.
Easier can a needle pass through a poor man's eye
than a gate through the Camels of Heaven.

**Better shape up, Buster!**

**There was a long embarrassed silence.**

*Perhaps,* **Larissa suggested,**
*we ought to consult at least one*

*Wise Woman.*

We chose Lucille.
She had experience with the ways of the world
including love, art, work, alchemy, money
children, ambiguity, medicinal herbs
and pain.

We found her in a foresaken gazebo
hurting from an automobile accident
neck realigned atop her spine.

*Ouch!* she said.
Which some of us thought
was not a notably wise announcement.

*Do your work well,* she added.
*Treat others decently*
*especially your family.*
*Watch out for crazies on the highway.*

**Everybody had special problems.**
**J.P., Linda and Carstairs took an emergency meeting**
**with the Estate's attorney, Melvin Jelly.**
**J.P and Carstairs argued for Big Diamonds.**
*They can be hidden,* **J.P. said.**
*They travel well,* **said Carstairs**

**Linda pressed for Real Estate.**
*Land can't be lost or destroyed,* **she said.**
*I want to stay home with my man and my horses*
*and work on my backhand.*

**But Melvin Jelly thought everyone was over-reacting.**
*Troubles blow over,* **he said,** *check your Bible.*
*I think our strongest position*
*is to hold our muni bonds, pharmaceuticals and defense industries.*
*When the market opens again*
*I'll recommend immediate acquisition of CarcinoTech.*
*Also conversion of 70% of our net worth into Swiss cash.*
*I'd be glad to handle the transaction.*

That night Marie fell asleep hugging her pillow.
She dreamed it was nursing her breast.

Then she dreamed she was unashambedly naked
in conversation with a Young Man.
Ted was his name.
He had blue eyes and spoke ardently
of tropical islands
and how beautiful she was.
He cupped a hand on her breast.

Marie pushed him away.
*That's for my baby,* she said, *not for you!*

*What baby?* Ted asked gently.
*How do you expect to have a baby
if you can't even be touched?*

Marie had to admit he was right.
But up close
Ted's face changed suddenly
into her Father's face.
Marie was twelve again and remembered
and woke up screaming.

I *suppose you use a wood-burning stove,* **a voice said.**
**Larissa was not surprised.   A long finger**
**of sunshine spotlighted a Young Redwood.**

*Yes, we have a stove,* **said Larissa.**   *Cold Winters.*
*But we never burn redwood. Too beautiful and expensive.*

*Isn't that cute!* **said the Young Redwood.**
*Bulldoze the Pine and the Oak*
*and save Redwood for pretty. Go ahead!*
*Chainsaw us into bay windows and toilet seats.*
*Soon there'll be nothing green, and no air.*

*My you're smart for such a young tree,* **Larissa said.**
*Don't patronize me,* **said the Young Redwood.**
*We all breathe the same air—trees, rocks, ants and you people.*
*Except WE refresh the air we use. You poison it.*

*Why right this minute,* **continued the Young Redwood**
*I can taste several molecules of acid*
*from a smokestack in Illinois.   Yuck!*
*And yes (sniff! sniff!), Brazil!*
*Oh God, they're burning the rain forests again!*

Larissa had never met so talky a tree.
She found herself asking what she'd always
wondered: Is it lonely to be a tree?

Are you kidding? said the Young Redwood.
We trees are a global family, in close touch.
Our language is spores, beetles, carbon dioxide, worms, birds.
We have senses you couldn't imagine. Sex for instance.
We don't need brains like yours to figure if we're ready.
You've read Freud. Can't you see each of us trees
is a permanent erection?

Larissa smiled.   You're boasting, she said.
Do you mean to say all trees are male?
The truth is—the Young Redwood began.
But a cloud crossed the sun.   The voice ended.

Larissa gave the Young Redwood a goodbye hug.
Its spongy bark against her cheek
felt for a dear moment
like the hairs on Rick's chest.

Rick called a halt at a fork in the road.
On the left was a Strange Woods.
On the right a Bridge.

My *maps don't show any of this,* Rick said.
*That Bridge doesn't exist.*

My! said Little Redtop
*I wonder what's in those trees. Perhaps some birds?*
*Where did all the deer and the rabbits go?*

*You better stay with us,* Rick called out.

*See you soooooon,* sang Little Redtop.
Off she skipped into the Foggy Woods.

She soon found a curious house
peeped through a window
and saw a Fool.

He wouldn't answer her cheerful *Hello*
or even look up.
*Sir,* Little Redtop insisted
*can you tell me where the birds and the deer have gone?*

Instead of answering
the Fool slowly dissolved into air.
Had Little Redtop imagined him?

She just had to climb in
to solve the mystery.

Whereupon the Fool reassembled himself.

Without conversation
quick as striking a match
he grabbed Little Redtop by her bloomers
and raped her.

*Why did you do that to me?* **said Little Redtop.**
*I hurt.*

**The Fool finally spoke.**
*Because it felt good,* **he said.**
*And why did you break into MY house?*
*I was curious,* **said Little Redtop.**
*I'm a naturally friendly child.*

*You're really a foolish child,* **said the Fool.**
*You don't know anything about men*
*or the world.*
*Go on, go home.*

*There is no home anymore,* **said Little Redtop.**
*You know that.*

**But the Fool just disappeared again**
**and stayed there.**

**Not even Rick could compute where we were.**
*My compass spins in circles,* **he said.**
*That's what happens at the North Pole.*
*But where's the snow?*

**After Little Redtop finally straggled in**
**all scrunged and teary**
**Rick made a speech:** *Folks,* **he said**
*the only way we're going to survive*
*is if we all stick together.*
*Including you, Redtop, hear?*

**Rick continued:** *We've got to*
*keep moving. My idea is we'll find*
*a safe civilized town*
*maybe just over that Bridge.*
*Let's go!*

**The road got narrower and nowhere-er.**

**By twilight we pitched camp
in a nest of deserted cars.
One of the children discovered
a huge grove of wild blueberries.
By light of a half moon
we filled our bellies with their sweetness.
Everyone's sleep was burdened with dreams.**

In the morning, though our mouths
were still stained with its juice
the blueberry grove had vanished.

An ocean or inland sea
had opened while we slept.
It lived on no map.

Rick tasted the water. It was salt.
*Hudson's* Bay? he wondered. *Sea of Irkutsk?*

The children had no fears.
Some found jewels.
Little Redtop insisted she'd seen a bird.

*Will you look at those wonderful rocks!* **said Julia.**
*We must study their meaning.*

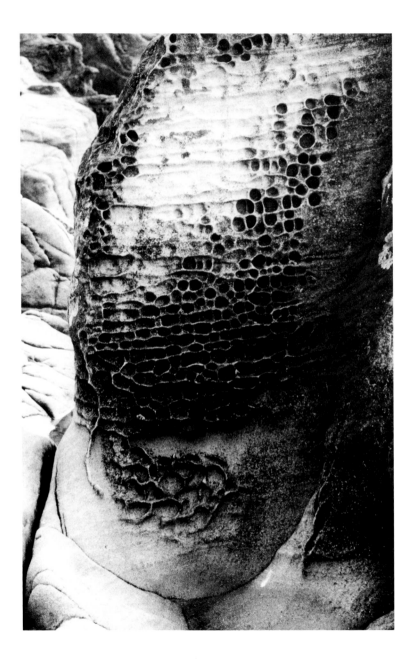

There's no meaning here, **said the Stranger.**
The world of nature is strictly facts.
Just geology, physics, economics
and slimey water.

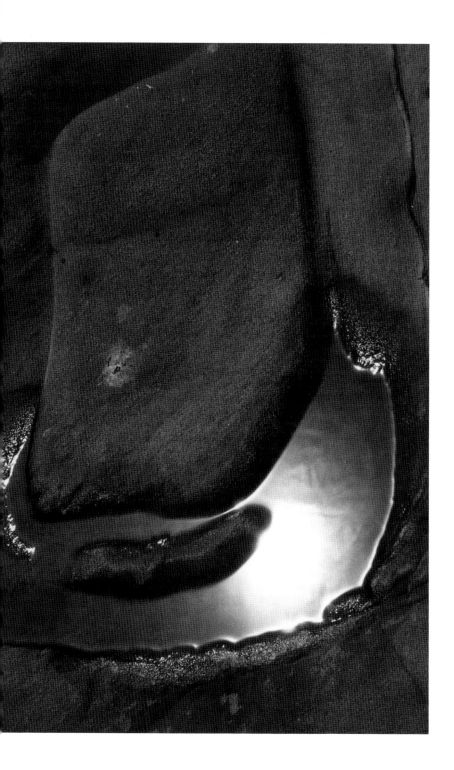

*Are you sure?* **asked Marie.**

*Are you sure about that?*

**For she knew she'd seen a baby in the surf**

**almost taken it**

**before it washed away.**

**Larissa found the egg.**
*Look!* **she said.**   *The map of Africa!*

*Nonsense!* **said Cousin George.**   *It's just a goose egg*
*some seagull sucked dry.*

*Eggs-actly!* **said Teshome.**   *Some European seagull.*

*Puns are fun,* **said the Stranger.**
*But truth isn't a joke.*
*You blacks always oversimplify.*

*Have you ever been powerless and hungry*
*for a long long time?* **inquired Teshome.**

Marie was afraid she was going crazy.
Life among the Changes was wearing her down.

All she wanted was her own family to love
which she didn't think was too much to ask
of God.

But all the men now seemed gay or scared or taken.




As for Cousin George, living on berries and fish
wasn't his idea of the good life either.
He'd been so sweetly close to his first million
when history hit the fan.

He missed the cameras and lights
his face on the screen.
He missed his tennis, his coke, his Malibu pad
his uncommitted access to beautiful women.

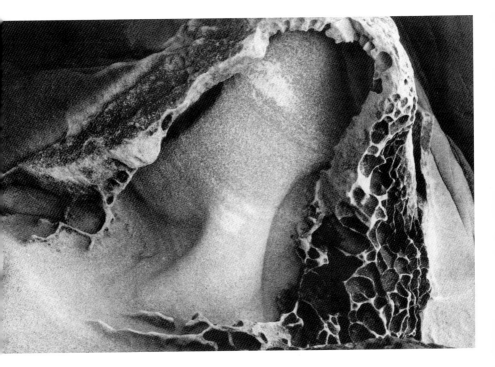

So it wasn't surprising
when Cousin George invited Marie
for a walk along the shore
or that she agreed.

Cousin George took Marie's hand
as they crossed rocks.
His helping arm
found
     itself
          around
               her
                    waist.

They came to a sheltered pool.
*Oh look, George!* cried Marie.   *Dolphins!*

Big fish, aren't they? observed Cousin George.

Dolphins aren't fish, said Marie.
They're red-blooded mammals like us
but with bigger brains.

Suddenly Marie came aware she was understanding
the squeaky Dolphin language.
It was like intelligent music.
One strong Dolphin leaped up, and smiled at Marie
and whispered.

It was then, the wrong moment
that Cousin George tried to kiss her.

Marie sidestepped and stripped off her clothes.
Cousin George's heart leaped up thinking it too was a
Dolphin.

But Marie
with a sudden new strength and beauty
swiftly arched her body UP   and   out
and
sharply
down
to join her great wet lover.
She was never seen on earth again.

Alice announced herself a Conceptual Artist.
She didn't paint, sculpt, write, act, compose
direct, dance, play an instrument or even photograph.
*My art is concepts,* she explained
*made manifest by my own body.*

Alice masturbated an entire Saturday afternoon
in a shop window on Melrose Avenue
had herself shot through a fleshy part of the arm
at a rock concert on the Embarcadero
and magically walked through a giant lookingglass
in Central Park.

Her line of cosmetics and designer jeans
was starting to sell.
She won a Major Foundation Grant
and a Rock Star Lover.

So it was understandable
when the Changes started
that Alice's statement to the media
was, *Sheeit! There goes my career.*

During our Journey Alice grew sad.
She found rocks, shells and friendship
with us
b-o-r-i-n-g.

She wandered inland alone
discovered some remarkable mushrooms
and got stoned.

Rick led the search party.
When we found Alice, the Stranger
who was a Professor and Art Critic
was ecstatic.

We mourn a great artist, he said.
Alice has achieved the ultimate masterpiece
Herself For The Ages.

Media is all, the Stranger continued.
Alice was the first post-post-Modernist to prove
MEMORY IS NOTHING BUT OLD NEWS.

She demonstrates we really are
all actors in a paper movie.
She was flesh
then stone
and now inked paper.

*That's baloney!* **wheezed Mr. Bones from somewhere.**

*I'm no actor in any kind of movie.*

*I'm real.   I'm sick.*

*Can't you see I'm dying?*

*This is an actual photograph.*

Suddenly Mr. Bones was gone
our ocean was gone, gone
and Sun burned through clouds
dappling a valley with green and gold and shadows.

Little Redtop laughed and clapped hands.
*Look!* **she said,** *bossey-cows!*

*Where?* **asked the Stranger.**
*Do you suppose whatever you imagine*
*becomes what really is?*

*How I hope so,* **said Larissa.** *Now look again.*
*Again!*

As if Larissa were a storybook magician
the veined spheres of our eyes
clouded over
till the whole world was only a luminous field
of microphosphor bursts
on a programless
TV screen.

*Look closer!* Larissa's voice said.
And then emerged not a picture but words:

### PETITION TO THE LEADERS OF THE WORLD

PLEASE REMEMBER THE ENDLESS QUEUES OF
THE HUMAN RACE, HOW WE STAND EACH DAY
WAITING FOR OUR RICE, OUR WORK, OUR
MONEY, OUR LOVE, OUR FATE. PLEASE ALSO
REMEMBER THE BLUE EARTH ITSELF, AND
THE POSSIBILITY OF YOUR OWN SALVATION.

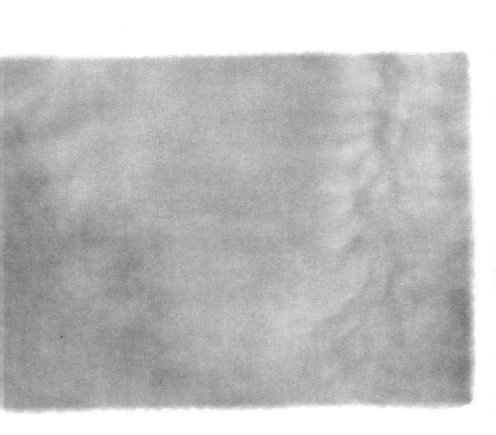

# 5 HOME

When we could see and be again
we all found ourselves home.
Had there been no Journey?
Had Larissa magicked our dreams?
Where were Tyrone, Betty Sue, Marie, Alice?

But there wasn't time to think of such things.
We all had to go to the bathroom
schedule the baby sitter
call our broker
gas the car (where WAS that car?)
see the dentist
phone the boss
check on grandma, the fridge, the mail, the lawn, the cat.

We were all hungry.
And I was out of film.

Virginia called, said she'd feed us.
When we got to her house
she sat mysteriously in air
entertaining the Stranger.
He'd already eaten.

Virginia served us all hot coffee, fresh bread
and a spicy omlette big as Tuolomne Meadow.

Then we all sat out on the porch
and drank plum wine spiked with gin.
*Just dandy*! said Cousin George, smacking his lips.

We watched the maples
burn red in autumn sunset.

*The world is round,* **the Stranger explained.**
*Just think, our sunset*
*is someone else's sunrise.*

*Besides,* **he added,** *our sunrise*
*is yesterday's Tomorrow.*

*I'm still trying to meditate,* **replied Alexandra.**
*I do wish you wouldn't annoy us all*
*with ideas.*

*Enjoy!* the Stranger insisted, passing around
macademia nuts, tangerines, condoms
samples of money, roast lamb on skewers
and small telescopes.

Rick and Leilani kissed.

What is to happen now is this gathering twilight?
**Larissa wondered.** *We all wait so hard.*
Will it be terrible?

**Larissa scanned the data fast-forward.**
*What was to be?*
**Memory and visions had always come quickly.**
**Now her mind's eye was slow**
**a vague pulsing of light.**

It grew to a time-lapse image, the fading of a rose.
Larissa had grown old too quickly.   Entropy.
Was accelerated aging the price for her special life?
Nevermind.   She considered the larger problem.
*Could there now be an Emergence?*

*Be of reasonably good cheer,* **said the Stranger.**
*Perhaps the best is yet to be.*

*No,* **said Larissa.**

The Stranger was at last exasperated
with this pushy old woman. *Look,* **he said,**
*you can't argue with sunrise, it will come.*

*Cockroaches will come,* **said Larissa.** *And the moon.*

Meeting at World Headquarters of the United Notions
in Beirut, the Supreme Leaders of the World
sneezed a Joint Communique.

Assembled in the great hall were 321 Prime Ministers
Presidents, General Secretaries, Honchos In Chief
and all their Staphs.

Observers included the Media, a Pope, an Oyveyattollah
an Imam, a Dalai Lama, a Rabbi, a Brahman, a Banker
a Beautiful Movie Star, a Military Hero, a Commissar
an Environmental Scientist, a Television Preacher
a Peyote Shaman and an Old Woman Who Carried
A Petition With Several Billion Signatures.

Each chair had a personal PsychoBabbleSystem
which instantly translated any spoken language
into any other. Everyone got an aluminum
Soviet ashtray with six Cuban cigars
and an American crystal ball
stuffed with Hershey Kissingers.

The cigars and the Kissingers went fast.

On the last day of the meeting
radio and television signals died
and PsychoBabble began speaking in tongues.

The Communique had to be cranked out in Arabic
on a hand-operated mimeo machine
and published to the world
aboard a hastily improvised hot air balloon.

According to the only two surviving witnesses
the balloon was seen to rise into greasy black clouds
where it disappeared, as Beirut itself soon did.

So nobody ever learned what the Great Leaders
had at last
too late
agreed
except perhaps the two survivors.

They were a pair of mutant literate giant Cockroaches.
It amused them to call each other
Adam and Eve.

The fallout from Beirut
and other cities
didn't spread everywhere right away.

Rick and Leilani found grass under a tree
and lay down, deeply tired.
*Remember that French novel?* **whispered Leilani.**
*I think it was Zola, where the coal miners
and some women get caught in a cave-in.*

*I do,* **said Rick.** *They were all about to die
and, being French, they fucked.*

Rick and Leilani's two smiles kissed.
But this night they held each other
innocently
till love and sleep
for an hour
rid them
of the
world.

●

## JOURNEY TO LAND'S END / A PAPER MOVIE

*Photographed on location in Carmel, Chicago, Hiroshima, Kamakura, Los Angeles, Los Altos, Malibu, New York City, San Juan, Santa Barbara, San Francisco, Santa Monica, Tokyo, Vandenberg Air Force Base and the deserts, countryside, seacoasts and mountains of Arizona, California, Colorado, Mexico, New Mexico and New York.*

**Producer**  
DAVID HINDS  
For Celestial Arts, Publisher

**Art Directors**  
LUCILLE BUNIN ASKIN  
MARISSA ROTH

**Creative Consultants**  
ANSEL ADAMS   JOEL D. LEVINSON  
SHIRLEY BURDEN   CECILE PINEDA  
CORNELL CAPA   CAROL TINKER  
WILLIAM GILES   AL WEBER  
DAVID R. GODINE   ELNA WIDELL

**Production Associates**  
KATHLEEN ARC   TINA IMAHARA  
LORETTA AYEROFF   SONOKO KONDO  
M. & L. CAMHI   NETTIE LIPTON  
DAVID GARDNER   TED ORLAND  
BYRON GOTO   BARRY SINGER

**Production Coordinator**   MARY ANNE ANDERSON

**Music and Soundeffects**   Imagined by YOU

**Representative**   **Legal**  
ROBERTA PRYOR   EDWARD MOSK

**Accounts**   **Publicity**  
ARNOLD LIEBMAN   DAYNA MACY

**Text**   **Main Title**  
**Set in Novarese and Gil Sans by**   **Hand Set in Papst Oldstyle by**  
GARRY AND CAROL HEATH   VERNON SIMPSON

**A Paper Movie Written, Photographed and Directed by**  
LOU STOUMEN

**LOU STOMEN.** Born Springtown, Pa.
Writer, photographer, forestry worker,
filmmaker, soldier, professor, futurist, poet.
Combat correspondent-photographer World
War 2 on staff US Army magazine *Yank* in
Caribbean, India, Burma, China. Flew on
first B-29 raid against Japan.

Two Academy Awards, five nominations.
Writer, director, cameraman, producer five
feature films, 90 short films & TV. Author
nine books of words and photographs.

Worked with Carl Sandburg, Aldous Huxley,
Walter Wanger, Winston Churchill, Orson
Welles, Edward Weston, Weegee, Slavko
Vorkapich, Marlene Dietrich, Lawrence
Lipton, Jack Nicholson.

Photographs, films and books in museum
collections worldwide. Doctor of Humane
Letters Lehigh University. Professor UCLA
film school 22 years. Three daughters, five
grandchildren. Home in California, and the
world. He photographs, prints, teaches,
goofs off and/or writes every day.